Blessed are your eyes, for they see,

and your ears, for they hear.

MATTHEW 13:16

✦ ✦ ✦

To my parents, who raised me in the Word of God and services of the Church.
M. M.

For my mom, who taught me that a prayer is a form of love.
M. A.

Published by Concordia Publishing House
3558 S. Jefferson Avenue, St. Louis, MO 63118-3968
1-800-325-3040 • www.cph.org

Text © 2015 Mary J. Moerbe

Illustrations by Martha Avilés © 2015 Concordia Publishing House

Manufactured in Shenzhen, China / 055760 / 300530

1 2 3 4 5 6 7 8 9 10   24 23 22 21 20 19 18 17 16 15

Whisper, Whisper

Learning about Church

MARY J. MOERBE

✦

PICTURES BY **MARTHA AVILÉS**

CONCORDIA PUBLISHING HOUSE • SAINT LOUIS

INTRODUCTION FOR PARENTS

Have you considered that one of the reasons we teach our children to listen to us is so they learn to listen to their heavenly Father? The small, ordinary ways we parent reflect the larger blessings of God. We speak, clean, clothe, and feed, and in a literal sense, we bring our children to church, where God comes to us. He speaks, cleans, clothes with the very righteousness of Christ, and feeds with the body and blood of Christ.

When little children attend church every week, the service becomes familiar and soothing to them. This book helps explain what is happening there so you can help your child learn to participate with respectful behavior and proper responses. Start by simply reading the rhyming text in this book. As your child grows, you can add hand actions or an age-appropriate lesson. And as your child's attention span lengthens, you can use the in-sanctuary tips (on pages 28 and 29) to further his or her understanding of the blessings and benefits of worship.

This book is not intended to be read during church. Instead, the most effective time to read it is during the week, especially on Saturday, to help prepare your little one for Sunday morning worship. You can also "play" church during the week—listen to a seasonal hymn, review the parts of the service in the hymnal, and practice sitting, standing, being quiet.

Use the "In-Sanctuary Tips" and "Teaching Moments" on the last pages of this book to help guide your child's learning about the worship service and about why we do what we do in church.

To make Sunday mornings go more smoothly, consider getting to your pew a little early to settle in. Resist the urge to sit in the back of the sanctuary and, instead, sit closer to the front. Toddlers are quieter and more attentive to the service when they can see the pastor and when there are fewer distractions.

Before the service begins, remind your child what to expect (sitting, standing, praying), what will happen in the service ("be good with our ears"), and why we come ("to receive God's gifts"). Practice whispering.

If your child is going through a noisy phase or if you have a child with special needs, you are not alone! In fact, by regular church attendance, you may be modeling behavior for the rest of your family as well as for others. Resist the urge to take your child out of the service (removal should not be a reward for the child). If anyone suggests something negative about your little one's behavior, a possible response can be, "God wants children to be in church." Such responses are also helpful to children, who may see various types of behavior around them and get a clearer picture of the Body of Christ.

Remember that no matter what is heard or missed in the service, God's Word strengthens you all. Squeals and cries during church not only send older parents down memory lane, but they also serve as reminders to everyone that the same God, present in His Word, is the God who gives, welcomes, blesses, and saves infants and children!

Truly, it is a beautiful thing when a child realizes that he or she can pray, sing, and respond along with the rest of the children of God! Even if your little one asks, "When will church be over?" you can know that as long as pastor is up front, there are still blessings to receive. Blessings from God last *forever*—even if you haven't been able to listen to much of the service. So church is never really over; it comes home right along with us!

Thanks be to Christ!

The Author

✦ ✦ ✦

Whisper, whisper, like the wind.

Whisper the /w/ sounds by blowing breath through the *wh* and *w*.

Hear the music. Let's begin.

Cup a hand to your ear. Make an open book with your hands.

Whisper, whisper, here God gives

Clasp your hands into the shape of a church; make a steeple with your index fingers.

All we need for faith to live.

Pump hands against heart like a heartbeat.

✳ TEACHING MOMENT

Being quiet in church shows
a reverence for where we are
—a place to worship the Lord.

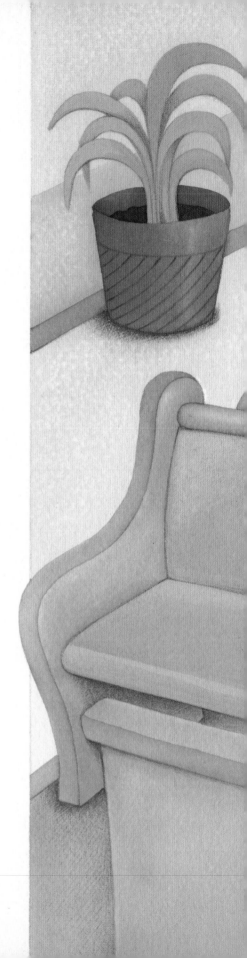

Whisper, whisper, make a cross:

Hold index finger of each hand to make a cross.

Forehead, tummy, side, across.

With two fingers, touch each spot.

Whisper, whisper, sing along;

Make an open hymnal with your hands; then, point to one palm.

Then, confess how we've been wrong.

Thump a thumb to your heart.

✳ TEACHING MOMENT

The sign of the cross reminds us of our Baptism, when God made us His own children.

Whisper, whisper, now it's time.

Point to your watch or to a clock.

Can you hear if there's a rhyme?

Cup your hand to your ear.

Whisper, whisper, Jesus lives.

Make a two-finger cross.

Listen now as He forgives!

Cup your hand to your ear.

✴ TEACHING MOMENT

**Forgiveness is a gift from Jesus
that we share with others.**

Whisper, whisper, now God's Word

Make a book with your hands.

Brings God's gifts so we can learn.

Bring hands together over your heart.

Whisper, whisper, standing tall,

Make a two-finger cross.

Pastors preach Good News for all!

Spread out hands, palms up.

✷ TEACHING MOMENT

The Bible is God's Word.

Whisper, whisper, say the Creed:

Cup your hand to your mouth.

Tell to all God's Word and deed.

Hold hands to make a book.

Whisper, whisper, hear us say

Cup your hand to your mouth.

All the work God does this day.

Point up, indicating God.

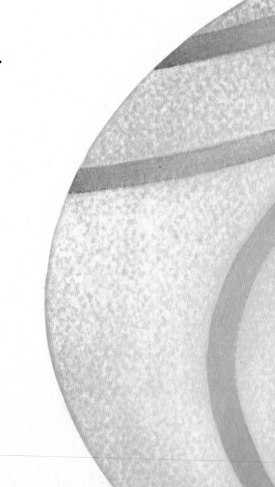

✳ **TEACHING MOMENT**

The Creed says what we believe
about God and all He does.

Whisper, whisper, sing a hymn.

Make a book with your hands; then, point to one palm.

Praise God for what comes from Him.

Point up.

Whisper, whisper, pass the plate.

Extend your hand as if to give something.

Give to God with happy thanks.

Point to your big smile!

* TEACHING MOMENT

God provides *for* us and *through* us;
God loves a cheerful giver.

Whisper, whisper, time to pray.

Point to your watch or to a clock.

Close your eyes with hands this way.

Point to your eyes; then, fold your hands to pray.

Whisper, whisper, say "amen";

Nod yes.

All God's children joining in.

Make a circle with your arms.

> ✳ TEACHING MOMENT
>
> We can pray our own words,
> someone else's words,
> or God's Words.

Whisper, whisper, now stand up.

Stand (then sit).

See the pastor, bread, and cup.

Put one hand at your brow in a flat salute.

Whisper, whisper, God is host:

Point up.

Father, Son, and Holy Ghost.

Make a two-finger cross.

* **TEACHING MOMENT**
**Jesus gives His body and blood
for the forgiveness of sins.**

23

Whisper, whisper, it is true:

Nod yes.

Jesus loves and blesses you!

Make a two-finger cross; then, touch child's heart.

Whisper, whisper, go with praise!

Extend hand, palm up, and indicate "go."

God forgives in different ways!

Place your hand on your heart, then hold hand out, palm up.

Whisper, whisper, you are blessed!

Touch child's heart.

God in Christ gives peace and rest.

Fold hands in prayer.

> ✳ **TEACHING MOMENT**
> God gives us ears to hear
> His Word so that our very lives
> are blessed!

Whisper, whisper, now we pray;

Fold hands in prayer.

Trusting God, show love today!

Place hands on heart, and then open to a giving position.

> *** TEACHING MOMENT**
> In church, we are reminded
> that God is our creator and giver
> of all good gifts.

IN-SANCTUARY TIPS

THINGS TO REMEMBER

- ☐ Children see better when they are sitting at the front of the sanctuary and have fewer distractions.

- ☐ Arrive early enough so your family can be settled before the service begins.

- ☐ Quiet toys, books, and snacks will reduce "action for response" behavior.

- ☐ Encourage "be good with your ears" so children listen to receive God's gifts.

- ☐ Short attention spans restart quickly and attention spans grow.

QUICK FIXES

- ☐ Discipline can be as simple as removing the problem and redirecting your child's focus to something else.

- ☐ Try correcting a child's focus by showing a two-finger cross and pointing toward the pastor.

- ☐ If you must take a child out, do not treat it as a reward. Remind him or her that we come to church to receive God's gifts.

VISUAL LEARNERS

- ☐ Before the service begins, ask questions about colors, pictures, and banners around the sanctuary.

- ☐ Ask him or her to watch the pastor's feet to see when he talks to us or to God.

- ☐ Bring a children's Bible and hymnal with you to affirm that children can participate in the service.

- ☐ During offering or a lengthy distribution, ask your child to point out a few things (crucifix, pulpit, acolyte, items on banners, etc.). This helps to teach vocabulary and offers a change of pace.

ACTIVE LEARNERS

- ☐ Leave a little wiggle space. Section off part of a pew with a hymnal, and allow hand gestures within the "strike zone" between shoulders and knees.

- ☐ Encourage your child to sit, stand, fold hands, kneel, cross, "play" organ, and "ring" bells at appropriate times.

- ☐ Have the child point toward heaven or relevant visuals when he or she hears certain words.

- ☐ Once numbers are learned, let the child find hymns.

- ☐ Consider a bag of sermon-only toys or activities so your a child does not tire quickly of them. As attention spans grow, have fewer, more mature options.

  - ▪ Consider your child's fine motor skills: zipping, buttoning, braiding, "sewing" a shoestring around a card rimmed by punched holes.

  - ▪ Let him or her quietly stretch, doodle, or look at pictures.

  - ▪ If your church has children's bulletins, let your child work through the pages and activities.

  - ▪ Let him or her color or look through Sunday School material again.

VERBAL CHILDREN

- ☐ Young children respond to cues.

  - ▪ Prayers and petitions end with cues.

  - ▪ "The Lord be with you" is a cue.

  - ▪ "Christ is Risen!" is a cue to say, "He is risen indeed! Alleluia!"

- ☐ To help with listening to sermons, choose one to three "words of the day." Your child can tap your knee whenever they are spoken or sung.

  - ▪ Start with nouns (Jesus, Savior, water); then, move to verbs (forgives, walks).

  - ▪ Try liturgical words and phrases: "mercy," "let us," etc.

  - ▪ Keep a list of words or topics on an index card that you keep in your purse or in the church bag.

- ☐ During the offering, ask your child to repeat names of people from the readings and add a little summary.

SINGING

- ☐ Refrains are often easiest to learn. Encourage younger children to sing loudly the parts of songs that they may know by heart.

- ☐ Having older children follow along in the hymnal furthers reading skills and teaches that all people in the pews can participate in the service.

REPEATING BACK

- ☐ Use your finger to direct your child's attention to go word-by-word for the spoken responses.

- ☐ Hold younger children and encourage older children to stand during prayers and other times during the service when the people speak responses. Learning this rhythm teaches children about active participation in the service.

- ☐ Lean close to your child's ear when saying responses so he or she will clearly hear the words you say aloud.

- ☐ At home, when teaching texts such as the Lord's Prayer, liturgical songs, or the Apostle's Creed, start phrase by phrase.

TEACHING MOMENTS

PAGES 8–9

When we're talking, we're not listening (and we may be distracting others). In addition, being quiet in church shows a reverence for where we are—a place to worship the Lord. But whispering is more than a matter of behavior. It also lets everyone use his or her ears to hear as the Scripture passages are read and as the message is preached. God teaches us and comes to us through His Word, the Bible. In faith, we trust that what the Bible says is true, and we receive Jesus and His gifts of forgiveness and salvation.

PAGES 10–11

The sign of the cross reminds us of our Baptism, when God made us His own children. You can also teach a phrase such as "God came down for you and me" with the same motions. When your child confesses something he or she has done wrong, you can say, "It is good and helpful to admit when we are wrong. God's Word teaches us what is right and wrong, and in church, pastors forgive us with Jesus' own forgiveness."

PAGES 12–13

As children grow, they are better able to understand the concept of forgiveness. Discuss: "Do we earn forgiveness? No! Forgiveness is a gift. Who forgives you? Daddy and Mommy, siblings, Pastor, Jesus, and others." Continue: "We are forgiven for the wrong things we do, but do we still need to learn right from wrong? Yes!" To help children learn that church is for all people, choose a word or two that is used during the worship service; when the word is spoken, read, or sung, your child can smile or pat you on the knee. Older children can keep a tally of the times the words are used during the service.

PAGES 14–15

Teaching specific words helps your child learn about the foundations of faith. For example, you can say, "The Bible is God's ***Word***. In the Bible, it is really God talking!" ***Mercy*** means getting help that we don't deserve. God is very merciful; God always hears us when we pray to Him in Jesus' name." Children know that words are powerful. Teach your child that God's "let there be" created the world out of nothing. God's Good News in Jesus creates faith in us and gives salvation and eternal life where it wasn't before! Sometimes, young children confuse pastors with Jesus. You can remind your child that God gives us pastors to forgive us, to teach us, and to keep us in God's Word! ***Pastor*** means "shepherd." Pastors help God's sheep stay together and well fed with God's gifts.

PAGES 16–17

If your child is older, ask, "Do you know why we say the Creed? The Creed says what we believe about God and all He does for us." Emphasize that God did great things in the past, and He still does great things in the present! God's Word comes into our ears, Baptism onto our skin, and the Lord's Supper into our mouths. Through these means, God comes to us to give us faith, forgiveness, and eternal life.

PAGES 18–19

Teach your child that God's Word is a gift we can share with one another every day. We receive God's gifts of mercy and forgiveness, and we share them freely. God creates us with unique abilities—talents—that we use to help others. Explain that our church offerings go to the local congregation, to missionaries, and to people in need. God provides for us and through us. All that we have comes from Him, so it is natural that we want to give a portion back to God. The reason we share these things is because, in Christ, there is plenty for all of us!

PAGES 20–21

Say to your child, "We can call God our heavenly Father because He makes us His children through Baptism. We are part of God's family because we are baptized in Jesus' name. Whether we are standing, sitting, kneeling, or lying down, we close our eyes and bow our heads to help us focus on what we are saying and thinking." You can also say, "Saying 'amen' is like saying, 'Yes, yes! Let it be that way! I want it that way too.' We can pray our own words, someone else's words, or God's Words. There are lots of prayers in the Bible, especially in Psalms."

PAGES 22–23

Ask, "What do we see at Communion? What do we hear? We see eating and drinking. And we hear that Jesus is right there, giving us His body and blood for the forgiveness of sins." Point out the elements of Communion that are shown on these pages. Then, point to the place in the hymnal when we "gather with angels and archangels and all the company of heaven" around Jesus and His gifts. Say, "We may not see angels, those who died in Jesus before us, or Christians around the world, but Jesus and His angels surround us. When we get to heaven, we will join in worship with all the believers who have died before us."

PAGES 24–25

Teach your child that God gives us ears to hear His Word so that our very lives are blessed! The Holy Spirit moves us to use our ears, hands, and mouths in ways that help others. Say, "God gives words to our ears and Baptism for our skin. Someday, you will eat the Lord's Supper. By His Word and Sacraments—Baptism and the Lord's Supper—God prepares us to see Jesus face-to-face in heaven one day." The word ***Christ*** means "anointed" (marked with water or oil). Teach that in Baptism, we are anointed and joined to Jesus. We are marked with the Holy Spirit through water and Word so that, no matter what happens, we are joined forever with Jesus. That way, He can be our peace and rest.

PAGES 26–27

In church, we are reminded that all good things come from God, the creator and giver of all good gifts. Saying the Lord's Prayer reminds us that God gives us life, daily bread, forgiveness, and the promise of eternal life. We trust God to give us these gifts, to hear our prayers, to love us through Christ, and to keep His promises to us. When we go to church to worship God, we are showing that we love Him and believe all these things about Him.